ROAD
TO
DAMASCUS

ALSO BY MARTIN P. KELLY

Plays from The Bridge

Two by Two by Two

A Cat's Tale

ROAD
TO
DAMASCUS

a play by **Martin P. Kelly**

Cover art by Mechelle Roskiewicz
Book design by The Troy Book Makers

Printed in the United States of America

The Troy Book Makers • Troy, New York • thetroybookmakers.com

To order additional copies of this title, contact your favorite local bookstore or visit www.shoptbmbooks.com

ISBN: 978-1-61468-631-6

DEDICATIONS

Richard J. Jones
1939-2019

This book is dedicated with love and respect to our dear friend, Richard. He was on the "tech crew" of our theatre "Riverview Productions" for many years, as lighting director and set construction. Richard's friendship, hard work and "can do" attitude made everyone's work easier.

In "real life", Richard was in the banking industry, rounding out his career by being in charge of Computer Operations for the Center for Disability Services. He was a devoted husband to Carol, his wife, and one of our finest actresses. Carol performed her roles with zest, humor and verve, becoming an audience favorite. Richard had four children, nine grandchildren, and three great-grandchildren.

Richard will be much missed by family, friends, actors & actresses, tech crew members, and especially by me, the Producing Director.

We are such stuff as dreams are made of
And our little life is rounded with a sleep.

Susan Kingsley Ingerson
1934 - 2020

A fine woman, loving mother, and a dear friend – farewell.

May flights of angels sing thee to thy rest.

CAST

(In order of appearance)

KATHERINE MALONE .... Parish housekeeper

ROSEANNE KEENAN .... Teacher at parish school

FATHER STEPHEN MATTHEWS .... School principal

FATHER PAUL CRONIN .... Church pastor

PHIL SCULLY .... Church trustee

BISHOP JAMES TIMMINS .... Head of Boston Diocese

THE TIME – 1970's civil rights period, particularly school integration.

THE SETTING is the combination sitting room and office of Father Paul Cronin, pastor of St. Jerome's Church, located in the southern section of Boston.

ACT 1

Scene One

At stage left is the entrance to the house, a two-story older home that serves as the parish house. A staircase at the right of the downstage door, leads upstairs. A step down leads to the combination sitting room-office. The office area is located downstage right, with a statue of Our Lady of Fatima with a votive lamp at its base, located up right with a kneeling bench in front of it. The entrance to the church is to the left of the statue.

(At curtain rise, the phone is ringing. Katherine Malone, a woman in her early 50s, the housekeeper at the parish, comes out of the kitchen, up left, next to the staircase, and crosses to the phone table next to the staircase.)

KATHERINE   *(In a hurry)* St. Jerome's Parish! Oh, hello Helen. No, Father Cronin is still at the church. He hasn't returned from the 8 o'clock Mass yet. I'm getting ready to fix his breakfast now. I'll tell him that you want to talk to him about the anniversary Mass music. I'm sure he'll agree with your choice. It's not a time for him to be thinking about music. (Pause) Frankly, I'm worried sick about it, happening only four blocks away.

Yes, I know some of our parish children are involved and Father Cronin is worried sick about the possible violence. Father Matthews has him worried too. He's an impulsive young man with a mind of his own. *(Pause)* Helen, I never bargained for this when I came to work here. I should have gone to California with Jane and her family when Tim died, but this area has been my home for most of my life. The friends Tim and I grew up with are mostly here. *(Pause)* I'm not sure anymore. This whole thing has caused everyone to change. *(Pause)* I know! Alright, Helen, I'll tell Father Cronin that you want to talk to him. Let's go shopping someday soon. Good! Goodbye now.

(Katherine replaces the phone, looks at her watch and starts back to the kitchen when the doorbell rings. She opens the door and Roseanne Keenan enters. She is an attractive young woman in her middle 20s, distraught at the moment.)

ROSEANNE *(Anxiously)* Mrs. Malone, is Father Cronin here? I must talk to him.

KATHERINE No, Roseanne. He's saying the 8 o'clock Mass this morning. Father Matthews said the 7 o'clock.

ROSEANNE Father Matthews will be down there when they start coming. What are we going to do?

KATHERINE Frankly, Roseanne, there's little we can do, except pray.

ROSEANNE   These parish children are all so young to be involved in this thing.

KATHERINE   Well, they're in high school, Roseanne.

ROSEANNE   *(Upset)* But they're so young to be facing violence. This past June, when they graduated from here at St. Jerome's, they so looked forward to going to high school.

KATHERINE   Well, they're still going to high school, Roseanne. It's just not where they expected, and not where their parents expected they'd go.

ROSEANNE   Their parents are so angry, I don't recognize some of them now. They've changed so much.

KATHERINE   Not all of them, but enough to make a difference, at least those parents with children who'll be bused to Roxbury, I suppose. I'm not sure how I'd feel under the circumstances. Jane went to Barker after she graduated from St. Jerome's and she liked it. She only had to walk six blocks. Now, she'd be bused about three miles across town to Warner High. I'm not sure I'd like that, nor would she. Thank God, she's graduated, married, and away from all this.

ROSEANNE   But what about the children who are still going to be bused out of our district once the buses arrive from Roxbury? What do I tell the youngsters in class this morning when they ask me about it? It used to be so much fun here at St. Jerome's. I've enjoyed teaching here. Father Cronin was wonderful to hire me after I got out of college.

KATHERINE   Well Roseanne, you were one of our star pupils here at St. Jerome's, and Father Cronin was proud of your work in college. He's felt very lucky to have you here these past three years.

ROSEANNE   No, I've been the lucky one! I've felt so safe and secure here. It's been like a family for me, a family I haven't had, really.

KATHERINE   I don't understand. Your mother and father have been wonderful to you.

ROSEANNE   Oh, I know, Mrs. Malone. They're wonderful and I love them dearly. But, being an only child can be a lonely experience. Now, the children I'm teaching at St. Jerome's are like having younger brothers and sisters I can help. It's been a whole new, marvelous experience these past three years.

KATHERINE   I guess that's what makes you a good teacher

ROSEANNE   But, now they're involved in such a terrible thing.

KATHERINE   It may not be as big a problem as they say it will be.

ROSEANNE   I don't know! I've heard these parents talking at a meeting last week, and it was simply terrible. People were calling for violence, using foul language and shouting at one another. They even shouted at Stephen … Father Matthews … when he tried to plead with them to give integration a chance.

KATHERINE   I know Father Matthews is deeply involved in this whole idea of integration of schools. In fact, he's in favor of it. He has had some long discussions about it at dinner with Father Cronin.

ROSEANNE   We've talked about it, and he can be quite convincing that it is the right and just thing to do, mixing children of different races. But when I hear the angry talk and shouting, I become confused and afraid.

KATHERINE   It is a confusing time. The things we thought we knew so well in the past, are not so clear anymore. I've lived most of my life here, and things didn't change too much in all the years I've lived here: the same shops, the same people, the same backgrounds and the same values. But, now there are a lot of outside events that have begun to change us. We've been living like on an island, and I suppose we think like islanders. But, what happens when they build bridges to your island?

ROSEANNE   It's strange but Stephen was talking about that just the other night after the young adult meeting. He said we have to build bridges between people as well as places. I guess we're all islanders who need bridges to one another.

KATHERINE   Bridges, real or symbolic, are difficult to build. I know! My father worked on one down the river 40 years ago, and my mother would worry every day about his safety. He lost two close friends during its construction.

ROSEANNE   Still, it was built. And so many people have benefited from it.

KATHERINE   But the construction period is a dangerous time, like now.

ROSEANNE   I fear for Father Matthews. He's like your father going out to build a bridge that could be just as dangerous. But, he doesn't have to do it.

KATHERINE   No, he doesn't. It's a civil matter that the police will have to handle if there is violence or any attempt to stop the buses moving between two schools.

ROSEANNE   That's what he fears - violence! And it's what I fear, especially after I saw the people revile him.

KATHERINE   They really did revile him?

ROSEANNE   They forgot he's a priest, or worse yet, don't care.

KATHERINE   It's something none of us should forget.

(Father Matthews comes down the stairs. He is a man in his early 30s, handsome in a rugged way, an athlete who has put athletics behind him. He is dressed in a black suit with Roman collar. He is a man who doesn't wear a hat.)

MATTHEWS   *(Greets the two women)* Mrs. Malone... Roseanne. Is Father Cronin finished Mass yet?

KATHERINE   He should be finished any minute! Do you want some breakfast?

MATTHEWS   Not right now, thank you.

KATHERINE   I'll get something for Father to eat after Mass. *(Exit to kitchen)*

ROSEANNE   *(Rushes to Father Matthews, takes his hands)* Stephen, you're not going to the high school?

MATTHEWS   *(Gently removes his hands from hers)* Roseanne, I must. There are so many of our children involved in this affair. And there are the other children, also.

ROSEANNE But the others are being brought into this district. It's not their school!

MATTHEWS We've talked about this, Roseanne. You know the justice of the thing as well as I. We have to face the fact that our public schools are a mockery to the whole idea of social justice. There hasn't been a black face in Barker since it was built.

ROSEANNE But, there'll be violence.

MATTHEWS Not if enough good people use their heads and treat this whole affair in a civilized manner.

ROSEANNE But, you know better. Look what happened at the meeting last week, they shouted at you. I heard people curse you.

MATTHEWS I heard them too, Roseanne. People cursed Christ! *(Tries to be light)* Forgive my comparison!

ROSEANNE It's not a laughing matter, Stephen!

MATTHEWS I know it's not. I'm sorry, Roseanne, for being flippant. I admit it, I'm nervous. I don't know what to expect.

ROSEANNE You know people are going to try to stop the buses. There's bound to be violence.

MATTHEWS I would guess there will be some attempts at violence. Hopefully, the police will be able to handle it. In any event, I want to make sure that the children are protected on both sides. I've got to believe that as a priest, I have some influence.

ROSEANNE   But you have our grade school to run, and spiritual duties that are important.

MATTHEWS   Roseanne, I'm well aware of my spiritual duties. I wanted to be a priest from the time in school when I served as an altar boy. *(Smiles)* While in college, I know I had a chance to play professional baseball, maybe even with the Red Sox, but when faced with the choice of a possible baseball career, I chose the cassock as my uniform.

ROSEANNE   You were lucky to be so sure!

MATTHEWS   Yes! I found the need to be recognized as making a contribution to the people beyond a stadium. The teaching of children that I do at St. Jerome's is wonderfully satisfying. As a priest, I like to think I can continue making a spiritual and a civic contribution to people throughout their lives and mine.

ROSEANNE   It would seem just being a priest would be enough.

MATTHEWS   But, I'm also a man living in this world around us. I need to be more than a preacher and a teacher. I guess I'm just foolish enough to want people to love one another.

ROSEANNE   What has love to do with busing students far from home to another school?

MATTHEWS   I would think social justice is an act of love. Not too many people see it that way, though.

ROSEANNE   Oh! Stephen, I feel close to all the things that we have discussed at our young adults' meetings, and I feel safe and secure there. There's no violence or threat of violence. But, when I come back out into the world, I lose that feeling of security.

MATTHEWS We can't hide from life, Roseanne. Hopefully, that sense of security you feel with the prayer group will remain with you and you'll be able to explain all of what's happening to the children.

ROSEANNE Until I do, I can only worry (*Extends her hands)* Look at me! I'm trembling!

MATTHEWS *(Takes her hands in his)* Roseanne, I have to go now, but I need to know that you will be able to carry on with your teaching today. There's bound to be some unrest in school with the troubles around us. Many of your students have brothers or sisters who will be involved at the high school changes, and they'll be concerned.

ROSEANNE I'll do my best. There may not be many of them there. A number of parents are planning to keep them home. Will you call the school when the buses arrive from Roxbury?

MATTHEWS I'll let Sister Monica know where I am if I don't return before noon.

ROSEANNE We'll all be worried about you.

MATTHEWS Have the children pray before class for a special intention.

ROSEANNE Special intention?

MATTHEWS Yes! They needn't know that they're praying for the children on those buses.

ROSEANNE I'll …We'll pray for you, too!

MATTHEWS *(Lightly)* I'll never turn down a good prayer. *(She attempts to embrace him, but he takes her hands, shakes them.)* I'll see you later at school. *(Exits front door)*

ROSEANNE Goodbye! *(Starts to cry, runs into kitchen)*

(Father Cronin and Phil Scully enter from upstage door which leads to the rectory from the church. Father Cronin is returning from Mass, and he has a surplice over his arm. He is wearing his cassock.)

CRONIN Phil, I understand your concern, and you have to believe me I'm as concerned as you are.

SCULLY *(Angry)* Then, why are you permitting this young priest to become involved in this busing business?

CRONIN First, he's not involved directly. He's simply monitoring the plans for the transfer of students to make sure that the children of this parish are safe.

SCULLY What was he doing in the pulpit Sunday when he urged the parishioners to give integration of the schools a chance? That was speaking in favor of the whole idea.

CRONIN The busing of students is an accepted fact, at least by the courts, and it would not be Father Matthews' place to speak against it. He was urging a peaceful reaction to it.

SCULLY How in the world can you suggest a peaceful reaction when the whole idea is tearing up our community? Why do our children have to be bused miles to another school, and in a black neighborhood?

CRONIN Phil! I can't convince you of the justice of the plan, nor can I truthfully feel comfortable with it. I've had discussions with Stephen ... Father Matthews ... about it. While he's convinced it is something that has to be done, I'm not fully convinced.

SCULLY Then, why don't you forbid him from participating?

CRONIN He's a free man as we all are. He isn't disputing spiritual values or canon law, so how can I, as his pastor, prevent him from involving himself?

SCULLY He's bringing disgrace upon the parish.

CRONIN Disgrace! How?

SCULLY Doesn't he understand that his immigrant grandparents and people from Ireland along with them, congregated in this section of the city and built homes and businesses, churches and schools. They did it all on their own, without help from others. Now a priest from this parish who also happens to be teacher in our grade school, is an activist in this busing campaign that will destroy all that was built up in the district.

CRONIN Don't we have any place for moderation in this world? Does everything have to be a battle where one side has to be the winner?

SCULLY Yes, if it's for the right cause. When you ask people to give the desegregation of schools a chance you're supporting the whole idea, like your activist, Father Matthews.

CRONIN I'd hardly call Father Matthews an activist. All he appears to be asking for is for people to consider the good desegregation will be for the children.

SCULLY There's good, and there's bad, and this whole idea is bad.

CRONIN Look Phil, I'll admit that I don't like the upheaval that busing is causing, and at times I have to admit to myself that the whole idea of segregation in schools or housing is wrong. Sure, I grew up in a world similar to the one we live in here in this parish. I'm familiar with this world, and I'm comfortable in it. But, when I discuss it with Father Matthews, it makes me uneasy, and there are times I resent it but can't say he's completely wrong.

SCULLY You can bet we all resent it. If you resent it, why can't you do something?

CRONIN Simply, Phil, in the final analysis I guess I am not convinced that this busing ruling is all that wrong. These children coming to the school are only three generations away from slave grandparents.

SCULLY And our children are also only two or three generations from slavery with their grandparents working as tenant farmers in Ireland where the English landowners took most of what they grew as rent. The Irish suffered famines as a result and on their own worked their way to this country to gain freedom from the English.

CRONIN But you'll agree that the schools where those kids are coming from are overcrowded schools that have been neglected without any public interest in repairs or renovations.

SCULLY   You wouldn't dare say that from the pulpit. You'd lose your parish, for sure.

CRONIN No, I can't say it the way Father Matthews has. It's strange that while I'm his superior, he is more free than I am.

SCULLY   How's that?

CRONIN My responsibility as a priest and as pastor is to hold this parish together. In a sense, I'm like a politician who must not lose contact with his constituents, or else I can be of no use to them. I need to lead them towards what is fair and just. Once you get too far out in front, you've lost your ability to lead. Followers must be able to see leaders in order to guide them to what is right.

SCULLY   How does this concern itself with this busing business?

CRONIN It's simple, Phil. If I were completely against the idea, and said so, it would incite greater disrespect for the law than we are now experiencing. It would mean the end of my ability to lead a parish towards the spiritual objectives that are my main responsibility. If I were to become an ardent advocate of busing, then I would also cause heated dissension, with the same disruption in parish life.

SCULLY   But you'd have strong support from your parishioners, if you told them publicly that you were not in favor of this busing scheme. Wouldn't that help you as a pastor?

CRONIN It might make me popular for a time, but it would not solve the problem. No, Phil, it's a great frustration to have to walk the narrow line, or to sit on a fence. It would be a pleasure, I think, to be a simple priest again without the burdens of being a pastor and administrator.

SCULLY You might get your wish sooner than you think, if this thing goes the way it's going.

CRONIN What is that supposed to mean?

SCULLY Well, the trustees of this church are people with children involved in this mess and if you lose their support in your fund drives for the school or church, this parish will go downhill, and you'll be transferred soon enough.

CRONIN Phil, that's a threat that doesn't have too much sting to it, given the present set of circumstances. But, I'm surprised, surprised and hurt that you would make such a statement.

SCULLY I just feel so damn strongly about this whole situation that I can't help myself. Look, I like this section of town. I've lived here all my life, built my business here and sent my kids to these schools where I went myself. Hell, you know very well that I could have moved away long ago. My plumbing business has been good. I could have sent my children to private or parochial schools, but I've stayed loyal to St. Jerome's, and didn't desert it like others did when they prospered and moved to the suburbs.

CRONIN And, we've all been grateful for your support over the years, Phil.

SCULLY But, one thing is sure. If these bus transfers take place, there'll be a lot of us who'll move out, and those are the church's chief supporters, as you well know.

CRONIN It sounds like another threat, Phil.

SCULLY Call it what you will, Father. It's no idle threat, I can assure you.

CRONIN What would you have me do, Phil?

SCULLY Have Father Matthews transferred.

CRONIN Phil, you know very well that I have no grounds to have Father Matthews transferred. He was one of the brightest seminarians to be ordained in years, and he has done wonders as principal of our school. On what grounds would you have him transferred?

SCULLY Speak out against this busing he's supporting. He's a troublemaker. Look at the problems he caused working with those dope addicts two years ago.

CRONIN What trouble? Complaints about a halfway house he tried to create for those people?

SCULLY But those people were drug addicts.

CRONIN Christ worked with lepers.

SCULLY But, these addicts were criminals.

CRONIN So were the lepers, in their day.

SCULLY Now, you're defending him.

CRONIN I'm defending him against unjust criticism. The things he deals with are controversial, so he's bound to cause hard feelings. But, it's no reason to have him transferred. Rehabilitating drug addicts is not a crime nor is helping desegregate the public schools.

SCULLY But the kids they're busing into this district have their own schools.

CRONIN Yes, they have. They are separate but not equal. They're overcrowded in the classrooms and even have to wear their coats and hats in class sometimes in the winter when the old heating systems break down.

SCULLY Some of our ancestors didn't have schools to attend. These black kids are lucky to have what they have.

CRONIN Lucky, yes, Phil but not equal. You heard how it was when our fathers or grandfathers came to this country. When they looked for jobs, they were met by sign: "No Irish Need Apply". Phil, maybe I don't believe busing is the final answer to the problem they're trying to solve, but I don't have an alternative to offer.

SCULLY I feel so damned used, Paul. I've worked with you closely over the last several years because you were my pastor, but mostly because I thought of you as my friend. I've taken time away from my business to run fund drives, and to solicit help for you.

CRONIN Phil, I've appreciated both your help and your friendship. It hurts me to think that you feel unfriendly towards me now. I dislike the unrest it causes because it galvanizes the hatred that pits one community against another.

SCULLY You leave me damned few alternatives, Paul. I'm really quite sick about the whole thing.

CRONIN I know that you are sincere in your feelings about this problem. I respect your opinions which is more than others might do, but I am upset that your feelings have led you to be rash in your attitude towards me.

SCULLY   It's a price we have to pay for feeling strongly about things.

CRONIN Maybe that's my problem, Phil. *(Katherine enters, followed by Roseanne)*

KATHERINE   Oh, Father, you're back, I'll have your breakfast ready in a moment.

CRONIN Katherine, don't bother. I don't feel too much like breakfast this morning. Just a cup of coffee will do. Good morning, Roseanne. *(Katherine exits to kitchen)*

ROSEANNE   Good morning, Father! Mr. Scully!

SCULLY   I don't wonder that you're not hungry, what with Father Matthews out helping send our children to all parts of the city.

CRONIN Now, Phil, we've discussed all that and we are not going to agree on the solution. So, why don't we drop it.

SCULLY   We can't really forget it. This Matthews will hurt us all.

ROSEANNE   *(Quickly)* He's a very fine priest, Mr. Scully, who has done wonderful things for the students at St. Jerome's.

SCULLY   Oh, yes, Miss Keenan, expensive things like rebuilding the gymnasium so a stage could be put in it.

ROSEANNE   The school didn't have a stage. Now it has!

SCULLY Yes, thanks to people like me. And what thanks do we get?

CRONIN Your work has been appreciated publicly, Phil.

ROSEANNE You know you once urged that the school be torn down, Mr. Scully, but Father Matthews got the people to support a fund drive to pay the heavy expenses of rebuilding it.

SCULLY Yes, young lady, but, who was one of the biggest contributors?

ROSEANNE You were, and the faculty is grateful for your help.

SCULLY We kept you in jobs, Miss Keenan. Remember that!

ROSANNE I can't forget it.

CRONIN Alright, I think that we've had enough of that for now. Roseanne, I hope that you'll give Sister Monica all the help she needs today to keep the children at ease during this crisis.

ROSEANNE I'll be going there in a little while for my art class.

SCULLY I would think you would. School has just about started.

ROSEANNE My class begins at 10 o'clock, Mr. Scully.

SCULLY I've got to get to my business. There's no one to run it unless I'm there. Father, please think about what I've said. You can't wait too long.

CRONIN I've thought about it.

SCULLY But, not enough. I'll see you later, Father. Goodbye, Miss Keenan.

(He exits)

ROSEANNE He can be abrupt, can't he, Father.

CRONIN Phil Scully is a good man, but like many of us, who don't find it easy to adjust to life's changes. He's rooted in his youth, and I can understand since I haven't shaken all of my difficulties with changes either.

ROSEANNE He really is antagonistic towards Father Matthews, isn't he?

CRONIN Maybe it's Father Matthews' directness of purpose that puzzles people who are not as young as he.

ROSEANNE I came here this morning to see if you could persuade Father Matthews from going to the high school. I'm afraid there are too many people like Mr. Scully who might hurt him.

CRONIN It's strange that Phil Scully was asking me to forbid Father Matthews from going to that high school, and now you're asking the same thing, but for a different purpose.

ROSEANNE I wouldn't want to see him get hurt.

CRONIN None of us would, Roseanne. But, as I told Scully, I can't really forbid Stephen Matthews from doing what he's doing, even though I share your concern. I fear, also, for his safety.

ROSEANNE We need him so much!

CRONIN We?

ROSEANNE Why, the parish, the children at school, and the young people who've formed the charismatic group. He's important to us all.

CRONIN I know, Roseanne. *(Katherine enters carrying coffee and cups.)*

KATHERINE Here's your coffee, Father, and some toast.

CRONIN Thank you, Katherine.

KATHERINE Where's Phil Scully? I brought a cup for him.

CRONIN He had to get to business.

ROSEANNE But, not before giving Father Cronin a piece of his mind.

KATHERINE Phil can be an angry man.

ROSEANNE He really dislikes Father Matthews, doesn't he Father?

CRONIN I don't think he does, Roseanne. He simply doesn't understand him. It's the curse of advancing old age. We lose contact with the younger generation. We forget our own youth.

KATHERINE There are things we'd love to forget.

CRONIN Why, Katherine? I'd never have thought as much.

KATHERINE   Father, compared to today's young people we were saints.

CRONIN I suppose so, but it's a world of heightened emotions and passions we didn't have to deal with.

KATHERINE   We dealt with a World War in our youth.

CRONIN Everything seemed so clear then, so black and white. Right and wrong had clarity. Now, there's so much gray area.

ROSEANNE   What's to happen to Father Matthews? Will you have him transferred?

CRONIN If I were charitable, I would! It would certainly please Phil Scully! But, knowing young people today, including young priests, I'm sure Father Matthews would find his share of problems no matter where he went. *(Lightly)* Why, they might even make him bishop someday, and then where will he be, dealing with young people??

KATHERINE   The young people, including priests, nowadays seem so involved in politics and social problems. What happened to the old days?

CRONIN The old days, Katherine? Young priests always seemed to be in trouble with their pastors. I certainly was.

KATHERINE   Tim and I didn't know you then.

CRONIN Monsignor McCormick was a wonderful pastor but deeply-rooted in the 19th century. When I suggested a spring bazaar to get funds for school sports, he was scandalized. The idea of a girls' basketball team really shocked him.

KATHERINE They are hardly monumental controversies.

CRONIN Well, to Monsignor McCormick they were; short skirts and all

ROSEANNE It's hard to believe a bazaar and a girls' basketball team would cause trouble.

CRONIN Looking back, I understand the monsignor's dismay. The bazaar introduced gambling into the school hall, and the basketball team ran counter to his concept of ladylike behavior.

KATHERINE We've progressed, and yet we haven't.

ROSEANNE Well, you could hardly match those things against Father Matthews' involvement with busing.

CRONIN No! You're right! But my involvement with Red Channels almost gave Monsignor McCormick a stroke.

KATHERINE You! Red Channels?! You mean the thing about publishing names of Communist sympathizers who worked in broadcasting?

CRONIN That's right! Seems like ancient history now but in the early 1950s it was terrible.

KATHERINE How in the world did you get involved? Was your name published?

CRONIN No, my name wasn't on the list but a good friend's was, a man who was just making a name for himself as a radio news commentator. His career and family were ruined because he interviewed people who were investigated by Congress as members of the Communist party. Many of his friends, myself included, made efforts to clear his name explaining as a newsman he had to talk to all political figures. It was a terrible time with many people looking at friends and neighbors with questions and doubts in their eyes because of the hysteria of the time.

KATHERINE   Certainly, your pastor couldn't question your help to your friend?

CRONIN He believed if my friend's name was on the list, then it automatically must be true... he was guilty! I was transferred after I led prayers at my friend's funeral.

KATHERINE   Transferred for a funeral?

CRONIN My friend killed himself.

ROSEANNE   Oh, how terrible!

CRONIN Yes, Roseanne, tragic. He left a wife and two children. Fortunately, his wife remarried several years later and his two children and their mother found a good family life, one without false accusations dogging their father. One of his sons is now a newsman with a California television station?

KATHERINE   Strange, strange! (*Starts to leave)* I've got to clean up the kitchen before I go shopping. Don't be late for class, Roseanne. *(Exits)*

ROSEANNE   *(Turns to Cronin)* I'm happy to know that you stood by your friend.

CRONIN I could afford to, then, Roseanne. I wasn't a pastor or a bishop!

ROSEANNE Why was there a difference? You were a priest.

CRONIN A priest finds that while it's no bed of roses in such a situation but a pastor or a bishop is in the public eye and must be careful. As such leaders in the church, they are not only priests who minister to the sick, buries the dead, begs for money, plays banker, deals for mortgages, consults with workmen and architects, and in the meantime, learns how to repair a balky oil furnace in the middle of a cold winter night. They really don't prepare you for those things in the seminary. Through it all, Roseanne, even with parishioners helping, it can be very lonely.

ROSEANNE Lonely?

CRONIN Oh, we have a whole parish of friends but they all have their own personal lives. Generally, we carry these problems all alone.

ROSEANNE It's the one problem I have with the Church's teaching. I don't understand the real reason for unmarried priests.

CRONIN (*Lightly*) Oh, Roseanne, don't wish the added care and responsibilities of a wife and family on me and my fellow priests.

ROSEANNE I'm serious, Father!

CRONIN Well, so am I, Roseanne. The Church in its infinite wisdom, has wisely decreed no wives for priests. What time would I have to devote to a wife? Where would be the fairness for a woman or children?

ROSEANNE   You wouldn't have to be lonely.

CRONIN I am not really lonely, Roseanne. I have my God to fill my solitary time, a decision I made a long time ago, and I've not regretted it.

ROSEANNE   But, a woman might want to help.

CRONIN Roseanne, but what peace would a wife have, married to a young man like Father Matthew with his desire to be in the thick of a social or civic problem.

ROSEANNE   She might have the peace of knowing that she's helping the man she loves by just believing in him.

CRONIN I suppose a man could always use that support. But we find it in our spiritual lives and the support of our parishioners, people like yourself.

ROSEANNE   Well, I would very much like to help Father Matthews.

CRONIN *(Cautiously)* But, you do by helping him at school, and by being a good teacher.

ROSEANNE   *(Caught up with emotion)* But, he needs more than that. He needs to be able to talk to someone about what he's thinking. He needs to try out his thoughts, to test his ideas on someone who loves him. He needs to have someone who would hold his hand, and comfort him when he finds the world seems too much for him. Stephen....

CRONIN Stephen?

ROSEANNE   Yes! Father Matthews has so many wonderful ideas to help the parish, the community and the city. We've talked so often about his ideas. I've felt so much a part of his life that I can hardly contain myself.

CRONIN (*Tentatively*) You seem to admire Father Matthews very much.

ROSEANNE   Oh, I do, Father Cronin! I do! I want so much to help him.

CRONIN But, you do, Roseanne, you do!

ROSEANNE   No, Father, I want to help him more, to be with him all the time,

CRONIN (*Taken back*) But, Roseanne, that's not possible!

ROSEANNE   I don't understand that. I want to be with him, to help him, to comfort him.

CRONIN Roseanne, I think...

ROSEANNE   (*Cries out*) Oh. Father, I love him so!

CRONIN (*Shaken*) I don't know what to say.

ROSEANNE   I'm sorry, Father. That was a terrible thing to say.

CRONIN I hate to think of love being terrible, if it is love!

ROSEANNE   Oh, Father! I do love him.

(*Door opens. Father Matthews enters, clothes spattered with mud and eggs*)

CRONIN My God, Stephen, what happened?!

ROSEANNE   Oh*! (Rushes to him, attempts to embrace him)*

MATTHEWS   Roseanne! (*Holds her away*) Father, I'm sorry about my appearance. The crowd was worse than I could ever imagine.

CRONIN Come in, lad. Sit down. What happened to you?

MATTHEWS   The first buses of black children came on time, but the huge crowd was waiting. They tore up lawns to hurl mud at the buses.

CRONIN Terrible, terrible! Were any of our parishioners in the mob? No, never mind, I don't want to know.

MATTHEWS   I'm afraid there were far too many of our friends there.

ROSEANNE   But, what happened to you?

MATTHEWS   The mob surged forward past the police, and spattered the buses with rocks, eggs and mud. A policeman was knocked from his motorcycle. I went to help him and was hit by the flying debris.

ROSEANNE   Were you hurt?

MATTHEWS   I don't think so. *(Katherine enters)*

KATHERINE   *(Sees Matthews)* Father Matthews, what happened?

CRONIN The mob at school was hurling rocks, eggs and mud.

KATHERINE   At a priest?! My God, what's happened to this world? Here, let me clean your coat Father.

CRONIN Katherine, please take Roseanne home.

ROSEANNE   No, please, Father

KATHERINE   But, she has to teach!

CRONIN Please, Katherine, do me the favor.

KATHERINE   Yes, Father.

ROSEANNE   Why, why, why?

MATTHEWS   Roseanne, please do as Father Cronin asks.

ROSEANNE   But, I want to help.

MATTHEWS   You've been a big help, honest.

CRONIN Katherine!

KATHERINE   Come on, Roseanne. *(They leave with Roseanne weeping)*

MATTHEWS   The police finally were able to get the children into the school through the back door.

CRONIN To what avail? How can children learn in that atmosphere?

MATTHEWS   They couldn't turn back. It would be worse the next time.

CRONIN How much worse could it be, Stephen? You placed yourself in great danger this morning. But more than that, you placed yourself in the position so that you could be assaulted by a mob, many of them our parishioners!

MATTHEWS   What was I to do, when that policeman needed help?

CRONIN Your action was charitable, Stephen, but he had fully-equipped comrades to help him. Meanwhile, you, a priest, could have been seriously hurt while bringing disgrace upon the people who hurled rocks at you.

MATTHEWS Father, how can you stand on the sidelines and see this happen without taking some action. I took no action against the rock throwers. I just tried to help a man who had been hurt while performing his duty. I'm a priest ministering to the wounded, as you did in the war. What is the difference?

CRONIN This is a volatile affair that doesn't need a priest present who's being criticized for taking sides.

MATTHEWS Good God, Father, what side can you take? I've asked tolerance. Give the concept a chance! I don't like the violence or the need for police any more than you do, but it seems inevitable. I cannot stand by.

CRONIN You have very important duties here in this church and the school that requires your presence. The busing is for others to handle.

MATTHEWS Father, I can't agree.

CRONIN I didn't think you could.

MATTHEWS We don't share the same views on the role of the Church in this present-day world.

CRONIN How is this different from any other time? We've always had strife, hatred, wars, and violence in some form. But, the one steadying factor has been the Church remaining true to its principles as a beacon for people to find their spiritual comfort despite physical hardship. The Church can't solve the world's problems. Other men must do that. All we can do is comfort spiritually.

MATTHEWS We're in a different world. This century is like no other in history. God has given us the wisdom to solve great scientific mysteries. With our knowledge and our advancements has come equal shares of frustration. The Church's role in past centuries was to comfort and bring spiritual guidance to a population which had family stability that was based on living close to the land. Our industrial development has made us more mobile, breaking up rural communities and creating crowded urban areas where family conflicts forced members to go elsewhere.

CRONIN I know my history, Stephen.

MATTHEWS I know you do, but you don't seem to link it to a changing Church. These people seeking new opportunities, and people uprooted from other lands and civilizations, need the Church more than ever. Not just for moral guidance or spiritual comfort but for social direction also. The experience the Church has had over the centuries should be brought into play now. We've been among the best administrators in history, the most adroit bankers and skilled landowners while preserving vast storehouses of ancient art. Who's more experienced than the Church to help now?

CRONIN I'm a simple man, Stephen, dealing with simple things. Your point may have validity, but it doesn't help me in dealing with everyday parish affairs. What benefit is it to solve a major social problem, if I lose the parish to its violent solution?

MATTHEWS My mind knows what you're saying but my heart turns towards those children in those buses, both black and white, who need all the help we can give them to understand.

CRONIN It's not your place to do it. I'm ordering you to end your participation in this affair. This is for your own good, that of the parish and for the children in our own school who also need you.

MATTHEWS I'm shocked that you would make such a demand.

CRONIN I regret that I must play this role, but you leave me no alternative.

MATTHEWS Then I must honestly tell you that I cannot obey. *(Starts to go upstairs)*

CRONIN Stephen, you are not to go to the high school again.

MATTHEWS I'm sorry, Father, but I must. *(Exits upstairs)*

CRONIN Stephen ... Stephen!

(Walks back to office area, picks up breviary, and begins reading. He pauses, looks towards the stairs, then walks to the kneeling bench, kneels, continues reading and is heard to say:) God, help us! God, help us!

CURTAIN

ACT 1

Scene Two

(About 1 p.m., same day; same setting. Housekeeper answers doorbell, Scully enters)

SCULLY *(Agitated)* I'd like to see Father Cronin right away.

KATHERINE He was called to the Bishop's residence late this morning after Father Matthews' involvement at the school.

SCULLY Well, that's exactly what I want to talk to him about. Did you see the noon television news?

KATHERINE I'm afraid I didn't!

SCULLY There it was for the world to see. Young Matthews being spattered with eggs and mud.

KATHERINE How terrible!

SCULLY   Not only did they identify Matthews with this parish but they had to identify some of the egg-throwers as parishioners.

KATHERINE   How could they?

SCULLY   That's what I say!

KATHERINE   How could those people turn against their own priest?

SCULLY   *(Angry)* I can understand that, but what right did those TV guys have to mention this parish?

KATHERINE   But, they were from the parish, you said.

SCULLY   Sure! Some of them were from the parish.

KATHERINE   Then, the television people weren't wrong.

SCULLY   I can imagine what the papers will do with this thing.

KATHERINE   You can be sure the story will be covered.

SCULLY   And, there'll probably be pictures.

KATHERINE   I'm afraid so.

SCULLY   Well, we've taken action to counteract this bad publicity.

KATHERINE   You have?

SCULLY   You can bet we have! I'm having a meeting tonight with the St. Jerome's parents' committee. We're going to petition the Bishop to transfer Matthews.

KATHERINE Do you honestly think you'll get much sympathy considering that Father Matthews was assaulted?

SCULLY He had no right being there! We're going to save him from himself.

KATHERINE That's a noble sentiment but somewhat transparent, isn't it?

SCULLY There's no denying we're against this busing and we're not afraid to say so. This man has given the whole idea more sympathy than it deserves.

KATHERINE All he's asked for is tolerance.

SCULLY Look, when people see his picture on television and in the papers, all those flaming liberals with no kids in school will all of a sudden be supporting this priest.

KATHERINE How is that bad?

SCULLY They'll hide behind the fact that he's a priest who's been assaulted. They could care less about his religion or the parishioners of his church.

KATHERINE This whole idea is more than religion. It's a matter of justice.

SCULLY What's justice? Isn't justice a right of those of us who have worked to build schools and churches and businesses by our own hard work and resources? Why are we so wrong in trying to keep the things we've worked so hard to build?

KATHERINE That high school is supported by taxes paid by everyone in the city.

SCULLY   How much taxes do those people pay whose kids are being bused in here. Our taxes pay for their school, and it's a good one.

KATHERINE   That's the separate but equal idea we criticized about the South, isn't it?

SCULLY   And what's wrong with it? Everybody's getting an education.

KATHERINE   And we all live out our lives - separate but equal. Strange, but I guess I supported that idea my whole life, haven't I?

SCULLY   Of course, you have! And what's been wrong with it? Your husband built a good business. Even though he died far too young, he was able to leave you comfortably situated. You don't have to work. God knows, you aren't paid that much here.

KATHERINE   No, I want to work here to help the parish, but right now, I wish I weren't working here so close to this whole affair. I feel sick about the whole thing. I wonder what Tim would have to say about this busing,

SCULLY   You can be sure he would have sided with us.

KATHERINE   I wish I knew. It's strange, you live your whole adult life with a man and you can't say for sure how he'd react under certain circumstances. *(To herself)* Wasn't I closer to him than that?

SCULLY   I assure you, Tim would have done the right thing.

KATHERINE I'm sure he would have done the right thing. But what would it have been? Oh God, to have known him and not to know him. How terrible!

(Katherine exits to kitchen as Cronin enters front door)

SCULLY Oh! you're back! What did the Bishop have to say?

CRONIN Phil, I can't divulge everything but you will be pleased to know that Father Matthews has been forbidden to go to the high school again.

SCULLY The bishop's a sensible man.

CRONIN Sensible, yes, but not insensitive.

SCULLY What does that mean?

CRONIN The bishop does not want Father Matthews involved in the busing program but he's not against busing itself.

SCULLY You've got to be kidding!

CRONIN No, I'm not. The bishop abhors the violence which has surrounded this program, but most of all, he is distressed that we even need busing.

SCULLY Does he expect us to accept this busing? To support him when he won't support us?

CRONIN He's your bishop, Phil.

SCULLY Not when he makes judgements that will hurt us. He's supposed to be helping us, the shepherd of a flock. Fine shepherd!

CRONIN Phil, control yourself!! Don't say things you'll be sorry for.

SCULLY And when is he going to make the big announcement supporting busing in schools?

CRONIN He's not! But, he is not going to condemn it, either.

SCULLY Well, he'll have to make a decision, one way or another. I'm meeting with parents of children from the parish who are being bused across town, and we're going to petition the Bishop to see us.

CRONIN You can't put him in that position.

SCULLY Why not? If he doesn't take a stand against busing, then we interpret that he's for it.

CRONIN He's for integrated education, not the violence connected with it.

SCULLY Well, he's not going to get the one without the other if he doesn't speak out against busing.

CRONIN He won't do that!

SCULLY Then, he's going to be reminded that he has just had his last successful Bishop's Appeal for funds. He'll get no more support from men like me.

CRONIN That's sounds like extortion, and you may be sure that it's been tried already by men with more weapons than you, Phil!

SCULLY He'll still hear from us, and I'm glad somebody is already working on him.

CRONIN Phil, I'm tired of the whole thing. It's been a long day and it's hardly half over. I have to rest awhile and do some paper work. So, if you'll excuse me.

SCULLY Well, I've got to get busy, too. It's a shame I have to leave my business to do the work our clergy should be doing, but if that's the way it has to be, so be it.

CRONIN Good day, Phil. Think twice before you tackle the Bishop.

SCULLY Good day Father! *(He exits)*

(Katherine enters from the kitchen.)

KATHERINE Father, have a cup of tea. It'll help calm your nerves.

CRONIN Thanks, Katherine,

KATHERINE Was it a difficult meeting with the Bishop?

CRONIN No! He's a wonderful man who has great compassion for those of us who are pastors. He was one himself for 15 years so he knows the problems.

KATHERINE And there are problems, aren't there?

CRONIN You have to be aware of a good deal of them being as close to the parish as you are. But, what you see is only on the surface. This busing is spectacular, but some of the less spectacular problems are as difficult.

KATHERINE Did you ever dream it would be like this?

CRONIN There's no preparation for being a pastor. Good Lord, if they ever started telling seminarians about a pastor's problems, there'd be a mass exodus of young men from the seminary. Who in his right mind would willingly follow a profession which might lead to this job?

KATHERINE   Still, it's a job to be done.

CRONIN But only with the cooperation of a great number of people, like yourself and your Tim, God rest his soul. Yes, and even Phil Scully.

KATHERINE   Tim did take an interest in your work.

CRONIN It was most helpful, even during his fatal illness. I could certainly have used it today. He reminded me of men with whom I served during the war.

KATHERINE   The duty that eventually took him from us.

CRONIN Yes, too soon! I remember when I was discharged from the Navy and was named assistant pastor in my first parish. Msgr. McCormick was a formidable man, but fortunately I had worked with some strict regular Navy officers, so I was somewhat hardened to discipline.

KATHERINE   As was Tim from his Army service.

CRONIN I'm sure! The Navy service quite often helped me deal with Msgr. McCormick's Victorian ways. But the Red Channels episode was terrible for both of us. The monsignor couldn't understand my loyalty to my friends, particularly someone who was being unjustly accused as a Communist. It was a blind spot he had, and nothing I could say would assure him. Fortunately, the bishop at that time, a contemporary of Monsignor McCormick but a man in tune with the times, transferred me to a chaplaincy in a hospital. Two years later I became pastor here.

KATHERINE   I remember it well. Tim had just returned from Korea. It was a difficult time for us. After serving in World War II and then being called back five years later just when he was getting started as a salesman for a large men's clothier, it wasn't easy.

CRONIN He was a fine soldier and sales man and a comfort to me during the time of the Senate witch hunt for Communists in the radio business.

KATHERINE He did everything well, and never complained. But, he was determined to start his own business with the money he saved while in Korea.

CRONIN It was a fine shop.

KATHERINE   And, we were forever grateful for your support of his store. We didn't know for months that you were sending people to Tim.

CRONIN I liked the way he did business and the way he made time for his church despite his busy schedule at the store even while helping his friend, the announcer at the local radio station.

KATHERINE He admired you, also. He liked your approach to things. You always listened. You still do!

CRONIN *(Light laugh)* It gives me more time to think of answers to an immediate problem.

KATHERINE   I prefer to think you have compassion for all people.

CRONIN I hope I do.

KATHERINE We need compassion now. I find myself confused by the Church today. As a young woman, it seemed so simple. Strict but simple. The changing Church has me baffled. They turn the altar around and now our priests become more men than ministers. The use of English instead of Latin takes away the mystery.

CRONIN Do we need mystery to believe?

KATHERINE No, that's not it. But, we need something beyond ourselves to look up to. It's so difficult to deal with things that are on our level. The priests dress casually, the nuns wear short skirts, and both run for political office. It creates men like Father Matthews in our Church.

CRONIN It gives us all more responsibility for our faith. We have to think about what we're saying in church because we understand the language more clearly. We can't hide behind a foreign tongue any longer.

KATHERINE But it makes us so individualized. We don't belong to the same community if we are all taking different means of praying.

CRONIN We all say the same prayers, Katherine, but we're just more aware of what we're saying, I admit I had difficulty with the changes brought about by Pope John but his simple approach seemed right when you give it serious thought. Maybe we lost some of the mystery, but it made us all responsible for our own individual souls.

KATHERINE Maybe it's more responsibility than some of us are prepared to take.

CRONIN Katherine, have you ever doubted your faith?

KATHERINE Truthfully ... yes! When you lose a man you love in the prime of his life, you question many things, among them your faith. Tim was everything a man should be - hard working, a good father, a wonderful husband, and faithful to his church. Why should he die of a heart attack at 49?

CRONIN *(Kindly)* Don't look to me for an answer

KATHERINE There is no real answer. Certainly, there is none without faith, and I didn't have sufficient faith at that time to grasp any meaning for his death except to know it was a terrifying loss.

CRONIN It shocked us all!

KATHERINE I took some comfort from your homily at the Mass. He would remain to all of us the perfect example of what a man should be. Age would never diminish him in our eyes. He'd always remain vital, cheerful, and devoted in our memories. It was some comfort, and I appreciated it at that time.

CRONIN I meant it, and I'm glad it was of help to you.

KATHERINE But I still felt so all alone. Gone is the strong hand to hold, the sturdy shoulder to lean on, and the ready laugh to cheer me.

CRONIN You must take comfort from his memory. And I hope you can take comfort from your faith.

KATHERINE It's the reason I readily accepted this job when you asked me to help you. I felt if I could stay close to the church, even in this manner, I could keep some hope of maintaining my faith. It's helped, mainly because I've been able to be close to you, and can remember the close association you had with Tim.

CRONIN You've been a great help to me, Katherine.

KATHERINE But I still fear for us all, and I worry about what this busing situation will do to you.

CRONIN It's a wise man who knows fear. Only fools aren't afraid. We've just got to keep the fear under control.

KATHERINE I'll try, I'll try. *(Smiles)*. Now, what would you like for dinner? We have beef stew, or beef stew.

CRONIN I think I'd like some beef stew.

KATHERINE I think you're in luck.

CRONIN Katherine! Thanks for talking to me.

KATHERINE I'm the one who should be thankful.

(KATHERINE exits. CRONIN picks up breviary and starts reading. ROSEANNE enters excitedly through front door)

ROSEANNE Father, forgive me for rushing in like this ...I...I!

CRONIN Child, I may never get my prayers read today.

ROSEANNE Oh, I'm sorry, but I just came from the high school.

CRONIN Why would you be there?

ROSEANNE I found it so difficult to believe what happened this morning. I couldn't believe people would do that to a priest.

CRONIN And, do you believe it now?

ROSEANNE Yes, yes! And, I'm frightened. There's an awful mob gathering at the school, waiting for the buses to arrive to take the children home. There's such terrible anger in the air.

CRONIN I know, I saw the scene on television. The bishop was shocked.

ROSEANNE So many of those people are members of this parish. Couldn't you speak to them?

CRONIN You saw what they did to Father Matthews. Why do you think they'd listen to me?

ROSEANNE Because you're their pastor!

CRONIN Roseanne, there's a committee formed in the parish to petition the Bishop to speak out against this busing. They're certainly not going to listen to me. I'd only incite a riot. I'd never be their pastor again.

ROSEANNE But, you can't be neutral on this thing?

CRONIN Roseanne, I'm not neutral. I don't believe in the separateness of schools but I'm not sure that busing is the answer either. The only trouble is that I don't have an alternative except a radical upheaval of our social system, better housing, more jobs, better education. They're solutions beyond my feeble efforts to achieve.

ROSEANNE   Is Father Matthews wrong in trying to gain tolerance for trying to integrate the high school?

CRONIN No, I can't say he's wrong. But, as a priest with other special duties, he creates a tension in the situation that heightens the passions. As a layman, he could do anything he wanted within the law.

ROSEANNE   But he wouldn't have the same impact as a layman. It's the fact that he's a priest that gives his views greater weight.

CRONIN And do you want him to continue?

ROSEANNE   I believe in what he believes but I don't want him back there where he could be hurt seriously.

CRONIN Well, you can rest assured that he won't go back. The bishop has forbidden him to engage in any activities involving the busing situation.

ROSEANNE   Thank God.

CRONIN Yes! Thank God!

ROSEANNE   That must sound strange. I believe in what he wants but I'm thankful that he won't be able to do anything about it.

CRONIN It's strange but human.

ROSEANNE   Father, is it possible to love a person like Father Matthews and have it not be wrong?

CRONIN Our Lord has asked us all to love one another,

ROSEANNE   But, I feel so close to him.

CRONIN It's natural, yet you understand that it can never be more than admiration of his work and appreciation of his friendship.

ROSEANNE But, there are times when I want to be so close to him.

CRONIN You know, Roseanne, that you can never be more than friends.

ROSEANNE My mind knows that, but my heart rebels.

CRONIN You will have to control your feelings for your sake, and for Father Matthews' sake.

ROSEANNE I'll try, Father, I'll try. Thank you for telling me about the Bishop's action. I feel better now.

CRONIN Then, go home and rest. We'll need you at school tomorrow. Sister Monica took over your classes today but she'll need you tomorrow.

ROSEANNE I will. Thank you *(Exits)*

(CRONIN resumes reading in his Office. Father Matthews enters from the Church, wearing cassock.)

CRONIN Stephen I didn't realize you were in church.

MATTHEWS I've been there for an hour or so, thinking and praying.

CRONIN Two worthy occupations for a priest.

MATTHEWS I guess I've been seeking some Divine Guidance on this problem.

CRONIN You know that you can't go back to that school.

MATTHEWS I know you told me I can't go back.

CRONIN It's more than a pastor and cleric now. The Bishop has forbidden you to go back.

MATTHEWS The Bishop?

CRONIN Yes, he called me to his residence this morning. During lunch, he told me that you were not to go near that school.

MATTHEWS But, the Bishop has been like a breath of fresh air in this diocese! I can't believe he would be against this integration of schools.

CRONIN I didn't say that he was against integration of schools. I said he forbid you to go to the school.

MATTHEWS Then, he's against busing.

CRONIN I'm not sure he's against it but he can't actually support it any more than I can. First, we're not sure that it's the final answer but most of all, the Bishop knows that once he takes a position, he polarizes the Church and will turn parishioners against parishioners, priest against priest, and worst of all, split the Church completely on what is essentially a political issue.

MATTHEWS It can't be a strictly political issue, Father. There's social justice involved, and the Church can't ignore it.

CRONIN The Church is not ignoring the larger issue but on this one problem, the Church has nothing to gain and all to lose. More importantly, the Church's support might even hurt, considering the reaction we've had so far, and the assault on you this morning.

MATTHEWS They weren't assaulting a priest. They were taking out their anger on someone helping a policeman who represents the power making this whole thing possible. They might even have hurled rocks at their own fathers if they helped a cop at that time.

CRONIN Your understanding and forgiveness of their actions is charitable and commendable but it doesn't alter the situation. You cannot go back there, and you are not to make any public statements on the matter.

MATTHEWS What you're saying is, that I'm silenced.

CRONIN That's about it!

MATTHEWS I suppose I should feel flattered that the Bishop should take such notice, but anger is a more suitable emotion. I am truly shocked that the Church could be so positive in its stand against one of its priests and yet, so negative in its attitude on a crucial social issue.

CRONIN Anger is a dangerous emotion.

MATTHEWS But a real one. I must talk to the Bishop about this restraint he's placed on me.

CRONIN You are not to disturb the Bishop.

MATTHEWS Is this your order?

CRONIN It's my request which I trust you'll honor.

MATTHEWS I'm confused by your attitude, Father Cronin. I've read of your activities when you were a young priest. You served in a war where men killed one another daily, and yet you walked a picket line with the shipyard workers and now you deny me the right to walk a similar line.

CRONIN The violence of war was thrust upon us, and our response to it was just terrible as it was. There's a scar inside of the soul for every man who died in my presence but it was something over which I had no control. My presence did not approve violence. It was, as I said, thrust upon us. And, when I walked with the shipyard workers, I was supporting the whole community. Their cause was the community's cause. Unless a just settlement was reached, everyone would have been hurt. The community was unified in that matter, and not split as it is now. The shipyard picketing involved everyone - white, black, Christian, Jew. There were no factions.

MATTHEWS Well, I don't have a safe issue with which to become involved. Our problems today appear more complex but we can't ignore them because they are complex, and not supported by the complete community.

CRONIN You're right, Father. The problems are more complex, and my life is more complex. My responsibilities deny me the privilege of being a rebel.

MATTHEWS But, I don't have your responsibilities.

CRONIN You're my responsibility, and as such, you must follow my order and the order of the Bishop.

MATTHEWS Is that what Msgr. McCormack said when you told him you were going to say prayers at your friend's grave?

CRONIN Yes, in so many words.

MATTHEWS And, was he right?

CRONIN *(Pause)* Yes!

MATTHEWS Yet, you prayed for your friend who killed himself.

CRONIN *(Pause)* Yes!

MATTHEWS *(Brief pause)* Will you excuse me Father? *(Starts upstairs)*

CRONIN Where are you going?

MATTHEWS *(Turns to Cronin)* To my room.

CRONIN *(Nods to Matthews)* That's a good idea. Get some rest. It'll all be clearer in the morning.

MATTHEWS Yes, Father. *(He goes upstairs)*

(CRONIN starts to read Breviary, pauses, shakes his head, appears to be confused. Housekeeper enters)

KATHERINE I thought I heard Father Matthews here.

CRONIN He just went upstairs.

KATHERINE I've cleaned up his coat. It took some doing but I got all the stains out, and pressed it.

CRONIN He'll appreciate that, and, Katherine thanks for being so helpful to us.

KATHERINE I confess I don't understand all that is happening but I want to help where I can.

CRONIN That young man will need all the help and understanding we can give him. We expect so much from him. We forget they are human beings with all the frailties each of us is heir to.

KATHERINE You know I'll help where I can. Did you tell him about the Bishop's orders?

CRONIN Yes.

KATHERINE How did he take it?

CRONIN As I would have at his age. He was shocked and hurt. Perhaps he felt betrayed. I hope not but it's difficult to reach inside another man's emotions and thoughts.

KATHERINE He's really a good priest, isn't he?

CRONIN Yes, one of the brightest to come out of our seminary. His zeal is a thing to behold. He has all the attributes to make an outstanding priest. I sometimes feel overwhelmed in his presence. He seems wise beyond his years. Yet, he has all the vulnerability of youth.

KATHERINE Someday, he'll make a fine pastor.

CRONIN And that'll be the end of him. Oh, to be a mouse in his parish house to hear him talking to a young assistant. God help us! I hope some of these problems will be behind him by that time.

KATHERINE There'll be new ones, for sure.

CRONIN For sure!

KATHERINE I'll take his coat up to him.

CRONIN Do that, thank you.

(KATHERINE goes upstairs. CRONIN resumes his reading. Shortly KATHERINE comes downstairs quickly.)

KATHERINE He's not upstairs!

CRONIN What's that?

KATHERINE He's not in his room, he's nowhere upstairs!

CRONIN Oh, my God! You don't think... *(He runs upstairs)* Stephen! Stephen! Stephen!

(KATHERINE exits, checks the church, while CRONIN'S voice is heard upstairs "Stephen, Stephen!")

(CRONIN comes downstairs as KATHERINE enters from kitchen)

KATHERINE He's not in church or in the kitchen.

CRONIN His cassock is on the bed, and his windbreaker is not in the closet. He's gone!

KATHERINE He wouldn't dare return to the school, would he?

CRONIN *(Winded)* I'm afraid that's where he went.

KATHERINE After the Bishop forbid him to go.

CRONIN Yes, even after that!

KATHERINE What are you going to do?

CRONIN I'll call Captain Williams at the precinct to ask him to head him off before he gets to the school.

KATHERINE   Thank God!

CRONIN *(Starts to dial 9-1-1)* Oh, my God! *(Drops phone, clutches chest, grasps table, starts to faint, crumbles to the floor.)*

KATHERINE *(Runs to him)* Father ... Paul, what happened! Father!

(CRONIN is moaning on floor.)

KATHERINE *(Picks up phone, checks Rolodex)* I'll call Dr. Reynolds, I'll call him, Paul. *(Starts to dial as curtain falls)*

CURTAIN

Intermission

ACT TWO

(At curtain rise moments later, KATHERINE is on phone with Dr. Reynolds.)

KATHERINE I wish he had agreed to go to the hospital, doctor. Yes, I know that you can't get him to do anything he doesn't want to do. But, he had a spell like this several months ago. The blood pressure must have dropped again when he found out about Father Matthews. Yes, doctor, I'll try to keep him in his room. I'll give him the medicine after dinner. You'll come over again tomorrow morning? Good. Thank you, doctor.

(Replaces phone, turns to see Father Cronin coming downstairs.)

KATHERINE Paul! Father Cronin, what are you doing?

CRONIN I'm coming downstairs, and I know it's against doctor's orders, but I feel better, Katherine, so don't be alarmed.

KATHERINE   But Doctor Reynolds insisted that you stay in bed.

CRONIN John Reynolds is a fine doctor, but staying in bed would kill me at a time like this, and he knows it.

KATHERINE   There's nothing you can do.

CRONIN Have you heard anything from Father Matthews, or about him?

KATHERINE   Frankly, Father Matthews hasn't been my chief concern these past two hours. Getting a doctor for you and making sure you're alright seemed more important.

CRONIN I appreciate your help, Katherine. Forgive the spell, will you?

KATHERINE   It's not your fault that you have low blood pressure.

CRONIN But, I've got to get a better grip on myself.

KATHERINE   These are unusual times. It's difficult for all of us to live normally.

CRONIN Just the same, I appreciate your strength at a time like this.

KATHERINE   I'm not as strong as you would believe.

CRONIN You come from strong stock, Katherine, the Irish women who saw their men off in fishing ships, and nursed them as they came back broken, or worse yet, mourned them when the sea claimed them.

KATHERINE You're over-emphasizing my help. When the doctor left, I called Jane in California to tell her of the things that have been happening. I needed comfort from someone close to me.

CRONIN Of course you do, Katherine.

KATHERINE Jane suggested that I come out to California and live there.

CRONIN Go to California?

KATHERINE Yes Father, I'm thinking very seriously about it. Life has changed so much here that I don't feel part of it anymore.

CRONIN I'm sorry to hear that.

KATHERINE It's not my work here, Paul, it's the upheaval in this city, and particularly in this neighborhood. It's not the same as when Tim and I first moved here. I know it's like deserting Tim and you, Paul, but Jane reminded me that life must go on, and the living have to care for themselves.

CRONIN There's no disputing that.

KATHERINE Jane is expecting her first child. So I have a chance to play grandmother, and be with the extension of Tim. Jane is a good girl. She urged me to stay with them for a while until I make a final decision, and get my own place.

CRONIN Katherine, much as I hate to see you go, I can't disagree with you.

KATHERINE No, I want to find some peace in my life, and these last few days have been traumatic for me. I guess I'm still living 30 years ago. I know I won't be able to recapture that time especially without Tim. But I can't live in the present here.

CRONIN I can't give you any hope that it'll be better. My guess is that it will be worse before it gets better, if it ever does. We seem to be losing our cities and there's little any of us can do to stop it, it would seem.

KATHERINE Maybe it's because we refused to adapt, to change as the years went by. We wanted to live in the present as long as it was the present of 30 years ago.

CRONIN We're all guilty of that, I imagine ... I envy you, Katherine.

KATHERINE Envy?

CRONIN Yes, I wish I could make a decision such as yours, as completely and definitely. My life seems one of indecision, of compromise between principle and practicality.

KATHERINE You have to contend with responsibility which I don't have, except to myself. It's different. You said so yourself.

CRONIN But the problem is that I feel as if I'm drifting, unable to be definite in anything. I seem to remain the same even though the world is changing. The church has changed, the world has changed, society has changed, but I remain the same.

KATHERINE You've adapted to change quite well, I would say.

CRONIN Outwardly, perhaps, but I seem to be fighting myself. I was a rebel as a young man, and adapted as I had to as I matured into responsibilities, but there is the nagging feeling that there is need for a bit more of the rebel to express itself.

KATHERINE We need sturdy men in troublesome times.

CRONIN I'm hardly sturdy. I feel adrift in my own indecision.

KATHERINE You don't seem indecisive.

CRONIN Yes, I do, but what value is it to feel for both sides, if I can't be decisive myself?

KATHERINE Why should you feel so guilty? Phil Scully is definite in his view as Father Matthews is in his. There's a need for decisiveness on your part, but that brings conflict because you see both sides and feel for both Father Matthews and Phil Scully.

CRONIN I don't know how to help them.

KATHERINE They each can talk to you where they can't talk to each other. You, and men like you, represent the hope that someday they may be reconciled. Without you, there is no hope. That's your value.

CRONIN But, it's so frustrating. All I feel is like I'm riding in a boat without oars, being buffeted by opposing tides.

KATHERINE Paul, you are not adrift; your strength is in your ability to see the need for compromise, for meditation.

CRONIN I appreciate your trust in ability you credit me with, but it hardly seems like a talent now.

KATHERINE I wish I possessed it. All I can do now is run.

CRONIN Don't regret your decision, Katherine. It is a decision that you can live with, and which will be right for you. I know it.

KATHERINE Thank you, Paul. I needed your understanding of my leaving.

CRONIN I do.

KATHERINE Now, let me clear these cups and get you some fresh tea.

CRONIN I'd appreciate that. I still have to get the police to find Father Matthews and keep him from trouble.

(KATHERINE starts to leave when the door bursts open and PHIL SCULLY enters.)

CRONIN Phil!

SCULLY It has happened, it's happened.

CRONIN What, in God's name, happened, Phil?

SCULLY There's full-scale rioting going on at the school. I just heard it on the C.B. in my truck. Extra police units are being called in. They're cordoning off the area.

KATHERINE Oh, my God!

SCULLY A large mob gathered at the school, I'm told.

They were there to meet the buses coming to get the blacks. The police don't have enough men there.

CRONIN What in the world were they thinking about, leaving the kids in school all day like that?

SCULLY I told you what would happen.

CRONIN Yes, you did, Phil. Except, there wouldn't be trouble if we followed Father Matthews' advice and give the idea a chance, even if we don't agree that it's the final answer,

SCULLY Well, at least he's out of it.

CRONIN I'm afraid not, Phil. I have every reason to believe that he's there somewhere.

SCULLY Good God, why didn't you stop him? You told me the Bishop forbid him to go.

CRONIN Yes, he did.

SCULLY You certainly have little control over your assistant, that's for sure.

CRONIN I'm his pastor, not his jailor. He slipped out of the house.

KATHERINE Phil, please calm down. Father Cronin is sick.

CRONIN Please, Katherine!

SCULLY What do you mean sick?

KATHERINE He had a spell, low blood pressure. The doctor was here.

CRONIN It's nothing, Phil. I just can't take excitement anymore, I guess.

KATHERINE He was calling the police to stop Father Matthews when he collapsed.

SCULLY I'm sorry, Father, I didn't know. But, you can see why you've got to get rid of Matthews. He'll be the death of you, and the ruination of this parish.

CRONIN My God, Phil, you make it sound like it is all Stephen Matthews' fault. He's just one man caught up in this whole mess, like the rest of us.

SCULLY Except, he's an agitator.

KATHERINE Oh, no, Phil, he's not.

CRONIN He went to that school this morning to protect the children.

SCULLY They have police to do that.

CRONIN But not enough, it would seem. He had hoped that a priest could instill reason into the mob's mind. It would seem that he's wrong.

SCULLY He's supporting the wrong view.

CRONIN Where's your compassion? How can you be so sure that what you support is the final answer?

SCULLY I'm sure, and everyone in this parish is sure of it.

CRONIN Then you know the parish better than I, Phil.

SCULLY I'm afraid that may be true.

KATHERINE How can you say that, Phil, after all the work Father Cronin has done to build this parish?

SCULLY If he doesn't get rid of Father Matthews and speak out against this busing, then this parish is ruined.

CRONIN Come on, Phil, I've got to believe that the Church is stronger than that or else I've wasted forty years of my life as a priest. Where in the world is the word "Christian" in all this talk? What happened to "love" in all this discussion? All we seem to be talking about is...

SCULLY I don't hate anybody, but I don't want something forced down my throat when I've worked so hard to build a neighborhood. Where is the justice for those of us who have worked all our lives to build what we have? Doesn't the church protect us too?

CRONIN The church certainly isn't trying to take anything away from you, Phil, and certainly, I'm not. I guess what we have to do is share what we have with others who have not had the opportunity to do what we did.

SCULLY But we worked hard for what we have.

CRONIN But we've got to give others the opportunity to work hard.

SCULLY Sure!!!!

CRONIN No one wants to give away things free of charge without any responsibility. Just give everybody the same tools, the same opportunity to work hard to gain the same advantages we enjoy. That's all each of our ancestors asked. Phil, you and

I, and Katherine here, are only 50 years away from scratching out an existence on hard, almost barren earth in another land suffering some of the same injustices that others are feeling right now in this country. Our grandparents knew that, and our parents did too, and welcomed the opportunity that this country gave them to work hard, and to show some fruits for their hard work.

KATHERINE   Phil, please let Father Cronin rest. This talking isn't helping him. The doctor asked him to stay in bed, so he shouldn't be talking to you.

CRONIN I'm alright, Katherine, but I've got to find out more about Father Matthews.

KATHERINE   You go back to bed, and I'll call the police. You can't push yourself this way. Phil, I'd appreciate it if you let Father Cronin rest.

SCULLY   I'm sorry you're not well, Paul, but you've got to let us help you get this parish straightened out.

CRONIN We'll see, Phil, we'll see.

(CRONIN starts to stairs as SCULLY follows. Door bursts open and ROSEANNE rushes in and collapses at CRONIN's feet. KATHERINE rushes to her.)

ROSEANNE   *(Sobbing hysterically)* They've killed him, they've killed him!

CRONIN Roseanne, what are you talking about?

ROSEANNE   Father Matthews - they've killed him.

KATHERINE   Oh, no!

CRONIN Good God in Heaven!

SCULLY Jesus!!!!!

CRONIN *(Crosses to Roseanne)* Roseanne, get control of yourself. Are you sure that Father Matthews was killed?

ROSEANNE Yes, I saw them do it! This is his blood. *(Shows stain on dress)*

KATHERINE My God! *(Cries audibly)*

SCULLY How did it happen? *(CRONIN crosses to phone, starts to dial)*

CRONIN I'll call the police.

ROSEANNE The mob began gathering... and shouting ... and pushing against the police, as the buses ... as the buses came up to the school... *(She sobs)*

KATHERINE Don't talk now, child.

CRONIN *(Into phone)* Captain Williams, please!

ROSEANNE ... then the police started coming out of the school with the black children , and the mob surged forward ....*(Cries)....* and the police started to push them back and everybody started shouting ... some people began throwing things ... *(Sobs)*

CRONIN *(Into phone)* George, Paul Cronin, here!

ROSEANNE But the police started bringing the children to the buses... and then, I saw him ... Stephen, he was walking with the black children... with his arm around some of them who were crying. Then, the mob began throwing more bricks and stones when they saw him. The police pushed the people back further and the rocks fell short of the children. They were getting near the buses and then I saw him ... *(Sobs, moans)* Stephen, was hit in the head and he dropped to the ground and lay still! The children ran, as the police began swinging clubs to move the mob back as Stephen was lying on the street all alone ... I ran to him and tried to pick him up but the police pulled me away ... they wouldn't let me near him ... *(Sobs, cries aloud).* They took him away! I heard them say ... "he's dead" ....*(She runs to Father Cronin as he hangs up phone)* He's dead, Father, Stephen's dead!

CRONIN *(Takes her in his arms)* Yes, Roseanne, he's dead.

SCULLY   Oh, my God! Who would do that?

KATHERINE   Oh, Paul, Why? Why? Why?

CRONIN Captain Williams confirmed it. Stephen's head was crushed by a brick. He must have died instantly, he said. Stephen was pronounced dead at the hospital.

ROSEANNE   I've got to go to him!

CRONIN No, Roseanne! There's nothing any of us can do for him now, but pray. You must get control of yourself.

SCULLY   Paul, I didn't like what he was doing but, by God, I didn't want him dead.

CRONIN Some kill with words, others with stones.

KATHERINE   Paul, Phil didn't want him dead!

CRONIN I'm sorry, Phil. I don't mean to hurt anybody at this time.

SCULLY   I'm truly sorry it happened.

CRONIN I believe you are, Phil.

SCULLY   If there's anything I can do, please let me.

CRONIN Pray for his soul, Phil! That's about all any of us can do.

SCULLY   Yes ... yes!

CRONIN Now, Phil ... I've got to go about burying the dead and comforting the grieving. I'm still a priest.

SCULLY   I'll be around if you need me.

CRONIN Thank you, Phil. Katherine, will you take Roseanne up to the guest room and stay with her awhile.

(SCULLY moves to front door)

KATHERINE   Yes, Paul. Are you alright? Do you want Dr. Reynolds to come over?

CRONIN No, I'll be alright, but if Roseanne needs any help, you might call him.

KATHERINE   I'll be upstairs if you need me. I'll call Roseanne's family and tell them she's here.

CRONIN   Thank you, Katherine. *(Katherine escorts Roseanne upstairs. Roseanne sees Matthews' coat on bannister and picks it up. She becomes hysterical again)*

ROSEANNE   Stephen ....Stephen ....they killed you!

KATHERINE   Come now, Roseanne, let's go upstairs. You need the rest.

SCULLY   Here, let me help*! (Roseanne moves upstairs with Scully and Katherine, crying. Cronin moves to phone and begins dialing.)*

CRONIN   This is Father Cronin, may I speak to the Bishop please. He's out? Oh! Thank you.

> *(He hangs up the phone as the doorbell rings. He goes to the door, opens it. Bishop John Timmins, a tall, erect 60-year old is at the door.)*

CRONIN   Your Excellency!

BISHOP   Father Cronin.

CRONIN   Come in, please.

BISHOP   Thank you. Father, you have my deepest sympathy. Monsignor Williams is at the hospital making whatever arrangements that need to be made.

CRONIN   Thank you, your Excellency. I have to call Stephen's parents. Then, I'll see them tonight.

BISHOP   You rest, Paul. They told me the doctor ordered you to bed. I'll see Father Matthew's parents myself tonight.

CRONIN   It's a terrible loss, your Excellency.

BISHOP   He was a fine priest, Paul. As you know, I questioned his zealousness in this matter.

CRONIN Yes ! I told him of your wishes and I added my own restraint, but he was a young man with his own mind.

BISHOP These are terrible times, Father.

CRONIN We don't need any further proof than what happened today.

BISHOP I came to do whatever I could to help you.

CRONIN Thank you, your Excellency. I appreciate your kindness but I have things that I must do myself.

BISHOP Whatever it might be, it can wait.

CRONIN Bishop Timmins, if those buses come back to the school tomorrow, I plan to be there.

BISHOP Surely, you can't be serious?

CRONIN Yes, I am! Someone has to take Father Matthews' place. I'll stand with those children as Father Matthews did today.

BISHOP Paul, I have to forbid you to do this thing. It'll only cause more bloodshed.

CRONIN John, Your Excellency! Please don't stop me from taking his place. I need to express what I've been preaching these past 30 years in some more tangible way.

BISHOP But, it'll not do any good in this instance.

CRONIN Maybe if enough men take a stand as Stephen did today, there'll be an improvement.

BISHOP You want to go, even after what happened to Stephen Matthews today?

CRONIN Because of what happened to Stephen. *(Reads from Breviary)* "They became furious and ground their teeth at him in anger... Then, they all rushed together at him at once, threw him out of the City and stoned him. They kept on stoning Stephen --and Saul approved of his murder."

BISHOP   What is your point?

CRONIN Saul stood by while the disciple Stephen was stoned to death for his convictions. He was the church's first martyr.

BISHOP   I know that.

CRONIN Then, Saul on his way to Damascus was struck by a sudden flash of light, and as a result changed his life, and his name to...

BISHOP   ...Paul.

CRONIN Your Excellency, I've travelled my road to Damascus and now I must pick up the work started by Stephen Matthews.

BISHOP   Paul, this tragedy has made you overwrought!

CRONIN I'm in full control of my emotions.

BISHOP   Paul, do you think you're the only one who feels frustrated at not being able to take more visible action? You've lost a friend and an associate and the church has lost a fine young priest. I feel the loss no less, Paul! I still must bear the knowledge that members of my flock may have caused this priest's death.

The shepherd's staff of my office is not a very effective weapon in violent times but it is a means of maintaining a firm stance and to support its weary owner. Paul, you have great responsibility as a pastor, and even greater frustration at not being able to take decisive action in this crisis. Multiply that condition many times over and you have my situation.

CRONIN I know, Your Excellency, that your responsibilities are enormous but...

BISHOP I'm quick to admit that I need help, help from men like you. You're strong, Paul, and your reasonableness is a foundation on which to find answers to these problems. The bishop's miter doesn't make me less fallible as a man in dealing with the complexities of the world. Would that all we had to do is deal with matters of faith. We need men like the Stephen Matthews of the world, too. Not for martyrdom, God knows, but to remind us that we are dealing with worldly matters.

But our positions, yours and mine, Paul, sets us apart in that we must guide, however imperfect, the man or method, so that there is good that can come of all this.

Unless we can bring about rational actions through our own reasonableness then Stephen's death will be a terrible waste of a bright young man. I can't promise you immediate change, but I promise you that I will not forget Father Matthews, or his goal ..... and his sacrifice.

CRONIN Thank you, Your Excellency.

BISHOP I know you've faced difficulty in your parish, and will continue to do so because this death will polarize the dispute inside and outside our diocese. I assure you that you will be a far greater use to your Church and community by being the reasonable man.

CRONIN That's a great deal to ask!

BISHOP Courage is not always restricted to those who charge the barricades. I assure you that it takes greater courage to be the buffer between violent forces. What I'm asking you to do is far more difficult than what you are prepared to do.

CRONIN I'm not strong enough to do that.

BISHOP Paul, don't throw away Father Matthew's death. In the next few days of grief, shock and indignation, you need to establish yourself as the beacon of reason from which all sides can find enlightenment. It won't be easy. I will not order to do this anymore than I would order you to do as Father Matthews did today. But, I pray that you will take the reasoned way to deal with this tragedy.

CRONIN I don't know, Your Excellency.

BISHOP Think about it! Call me in the morning. Rest tonight! You have much to do. Now, I must go, as I also have work to do.

CRONIN Thank you for coming. Good night, Your Excellency. *(At door, he kneels to kiss the Bishop's ring, Timmins lifts Cronin up and embraces him. He exits)*

(Cronin walks back to the desk, and glances at the Breviary. Kathleen and Scully come downstairs)

KATHLEEN Roseanne is asleep. Doctor Reynolds said I could give her one of my sleeping pills.

SCULLY Father, I'll be going now. I'm terribly sorry. Please call me if there's anything I can do.

CRONIN *(Beat)* Phil, your meeting tonight!

SCULLY I don't think there's much point for a meeting tonight.

CRONIN It's even more important now. Phil! I plan to be at that meeting tonight.

KATHLEEN Father, Doctor Reynolds said.......

SCULLY Father, there's no need for a meeting. Emotions will be too high.

CRONIN Phil, if you want to help, hold that meeting tonight and give me an opportunity to speak.

SCULLY *(Pause)* Yes, Father.

KATHLEEN I don't understand.

CRONIN I have a road to walk, Kathleen, and it's time for me to start.

(She watches him as he approaches kneeling bench as he opens his breviary.)

CURTAIN – END OF PLAY